You Won't Ever Be the Same

Previous Vantage Press title by the author:

Don't Forget to Pray, 2003

You Won't Ever Be the Same

Joan M. Green

VANTAGE PRESS
New York

FIRST EDITION

All rights reserved, including the right of
reproduction in whole or in part in any form.

Copyright © 2005 by Joan M. Green

Published by Vantage Press, Inc.
419 Park Ave. South, New York, NY 10016

Manufactured in the United States of America
ISBN: 0-533-15066-3

Library of Congress Catalog Card No.: 2004097648

0 9 8 7 6 5 4 3 2 1

Contents

Preface ix

You Won't Ever Be the Same 1
Godly Success 3
To Tithe 5
Ever Mighty 7
A New Phrase 9
Sweet Eternity 11
Savior of Souls 13
The Homecoming 15
The Penny Jar 17
Condemnation 19
Jesus Can 21
Arrest a Fall 23
Our Talks 25
Unlocked 27
Splendor 28
No Exits 29
A Home in Hell 30
No More Fears 32
The Best Food 34
Depart with Pride 36
The Trade 38
Forget Me Not 40
The Quenching 41
What Sin? 42
The Godly Way 44
Finality 45
Without a Trace 47
Higher Learning 49
Call His Name 50
The Lord's Work 52
Her Change 54
The Lord's Paradise 56
Unimportant Things 58
Someone Sees 60

Don't Cry	62
Grateful	64
In My Dreams	65
Without God	67
Scientific	69
Until My Dying Day	71
They Must Turn	72
Directions for Salvation	73
Alzheimer's	75
An Angry Child	76
The Opposition	78
Half-Stepping	79
The Double-Edged Sword	81
Christ Tabernacle	83
Life	84
The Undoing	86
The Path	87
Never Missed	89
Take Heed	91
The Devil's Trap	92
Forewarned	94
Rebuke the Sin	96
Decide	97
The Sermon	99
The Party	101
The Blemish	103
Take a Stand	105
Immorality	107
God's Right	109
God Chose You	111
My New Agent	113
I Don't Know You	115
A Victor's Song	117
Divine Intervention	119
Words of Faith	120
The News Is Good	121
The Volunteer	122
Encouragement	123

Love Professed	124
Upstairs	125
Saving Grace	126
A Wonderful Day	128
Child of Light	130
Technology	131
About the Author	133

Preface

In the life we have all been blessed with, there are always obstacles and trials. However, if we walk on the lighted path which Jesus Christ has provided us, there may be trials but the Lord will always be there, encouraging, loving, mentoring, embracing, directing.

The poems you will find herein are written with the same purpose. They are written with love and compassion for my fellow human beings, they are written to address the human condition.

These poems are gifts to me, from the most high God. And I am very privileged to be able to share them with you.

I now dedicate this book to my almighty God, my Lord and Savior Jesus Christ, and in loving memory of my mom and dad, Lucille and Joseph Robinson.

(A Hint to the Wise)
The Master is on His Way Back Home; ARE YOU READY?

You Won't Ever Be the Same

When Jesus enters
You'll be changed
A slow process for some, it's true
But you won't ever be the same

For the Lord's Love
It will change you
Your looks and attitude
Will change

Your body odor alternates
The things you used to do
You won't
For you'll no longer have the taste

Study the Bible
And you'll glow
The holy spirit, invades you
The holy story you will know

You'll learn of love
And love that's true
Then as you mature in the faith
Your job on God's green earth will be

To spread the good news
Every day
Teach of the holy trinity
Yes you will change and
Change for good

The way you think and talk
And pray
For God will spread his love and light
To every bone and cell
Each day

Then you'll be blessed in the Lord's sight
As instrument of love and grace
Then as a Christian, join the fight
To put the devil, in his place

Godly Success

Some folks will say, "She's just a nurse
She is not scholarly
And yet she has, published a book
Of gospel poetry."

They say, "Who does this women know?"
Who gives to her advice?
My answer is, it's all because
I now know, Jesus Christ!

That day, when Jesus came to me
He took my hand and said
"You must give up the sin and shame"
And follow me, instead

Then I took off my cloak of sin
And cast it to the side
For I so wanted to be cleansed
To the scriptures, abide

Now I walk on a well lit path
And Jesus leads the way
He is my light, my guide my friend
He's with me every day

So if you're wondering just how
I was able to succeed
Pick up the Holy Bible, folks
And take the time to read

With God all things are possible
So with his grace and help
I wrote a book, praising his name
I'm so proud of myself

My Lord is wondrous, and good
With him I cannot fail
So learn his word, his will, his way
And to you, he will avail

To Tithe

The good Lord sees that you are
Working, each and every day
A job that you can go to
And each week, collect your pay

He provides you with a home
A roof, you also get three squares
But when the Father needs you most
With him, you will not share

For he only asks for ten percent
Of our wages or our gross
Because his house, it now crumbles
Like a well done piece of toast

He wants us to tithe in good faith
As many of us can
But some folks think this is too much
To ask of any man

The church must be supported
By the faithful , everywhere
But when it's time to help the Lord
Most of us, are not there

And yet we expect blessings
From the Lord, to rain on down
With the Lord's church now in disrepair
There's no blessings to be found

Dig deep into your pockets
Give our Lord God, His just due
If you hide your wallet, from the Lord
He will hide His face from you

For the blessings He may have for you
He will keep them all in store
So folks, ante up and pay the Lord
There is no need to say more

Ever Mighty

Jesus Christ, he was no joke
He did not mince his words
He spoke up with assertiveness
And made sure he was heard

The Pharisees and Sadducees
Were called vipers and snakes
For Jesus never bit his tongue
He put them in their place

He told them they were all blind guides
Sa-tan's minims and elves
Who kept their flocks from heaven
For they will not go themselves

They watched him heal
Raise up the dead
And give to the blind sight
But they would not acknowledge

He was the bringer of light
The one and true messiah
Come to earth, the son of God
So they said he was possessed

And his good works were facades
And when he forgave sin
They'd ask, by what authority
They'd criticize his every word
For he was almighty

Then they would crucify his body
But his spirit and His soul
They ascended straight to heaven
For the Lord, had reached his goal

Now all over this whole planet
He is worshiped and revered
For he is the Lord and savior
Ever mighty loved and feared

A New Phrase

What can I say, about Jesus
That you folks, haven't all ready heard
Just what can I say, of this most precious lamb
I must seek a new phrase, a new word

What can I say of my father
Because my Lord, is beyond compare
No mortal words can do him justice
And I want to be gracious and fair

As the presence of God
Moves around in my heart
I am bathed with light, and I am filled
Now I long to say something

That no one has said
Because it is my quest, and my will
I know he's my redeemer
My savior my all

By his blood and his stripes
I am healed
So I want to say something
Especially kind
While the Lord, still works out
In the field.

When the master returns
He will find my art work
In a poem filled with worship and awe
And I pray that my words

Fill his heart with great joy
If they do, I can ask nothing more
He's the true bread of life
The perpetual spring
What I'll say about him
Is that he is all things

If this poem makes him smile
My prayers are realized
I'll find eternal peace
And find grace, in God's eyes

Sweet Eternity

Near the mountains of heaven
In the valley of gold
Is now where you reside
In a mansion, we're told

You are there now as one
Where there is no more time
Now your love lives forever
And your lives, are sublime

Know, we all miss you both
And the Lord he is just
He gave us, you as parents
Now in God we will trust

Through the good and the bad
You were both always there
With a smile and a song
We just knew, that you cared

And as long as we breathe
With our memories intact
We'll remember the love
We'll remember the fact

That we were truly blessed
To have parents like you
You are both sorely missed
But we're not feeling blue

For we know that the Lord
Has you both in his arms
You're now safe and secure
Free of strife, free from storms

Now rest on, our dear ones
And enjoy, you're now free
For you live with the Lord
In sweet eternity.

Written in loving memory of our parents, Lucille and Joseph Robinson

Savior of Souls

I never pray to Mary
She was not crucified
It was her blessed son Jesus
Nailed to that cross to die

Then he was resurrected
I pay homage to him
He is my heart, for he alone
Saved mankind, from their sins

I will see him in glory
For he's the king of kings
Yes, by his blood and by his stripes
All healing he doth bring

Mary, the blessed virgin
She was revered by all
For she gave birth to Jesus Christ
A fete that was not small

But Jesus Christ he raised the dead
He fed the poor, with fish and bread
He stopped the flow of blood, from one
And helped the blind, to see the sun

He cast out demons, preached, and prayed
He taught folks not to
Be afraid
He was a gentle loving soul
To save mankind, it was his goal

So, people when you kneel to pray
Remember Jesus saved the day
And God the Father sacrificed
His only child, the Lord, the Christ

We praise and pray to only one
The Father, holy ghost, and son
There's no one else who paid the cost
Of saving souls, upon that cross

The Homecoming

I tell you, the master is on his way home
He is coming in fury
He will not be alone
Every angel in heaven

Will give him an assist
Gathering up every sinner
So that none will be missed
He will be separating

The goats from the lambs
For he knows the imposters
And he knows every scam
Like the bridesmaids, with lamps

That did not carry fuel
He will stamp out the wicked
Do away with the cruel
For the one's that refused to

Acknowledge his name
The'll be anguish and horror
Introduced to their game
The'll be weeping and wailing

And gnashing of teeth
For the wicked and wretched
There will be no relief
Right into outer darkness

The'll be all thrown away
And believe me folks, you will
Remember that day
If you're out in a field

Don't run home for a coat
For your chances of making it
Will be remote
If someone says to you

Jesus is over there
Don't go looking, for you will
Return in despair

So folks, listen to me
And to what I must say
For the master he could return
Home any day.

Get your business in order
For you must be prepared
You will not know the time
That the sheep will be sheared.

The Penny Jar

The child's brother had a tumor
Growing deep inside his brain
And her parents, they were worried
And under, tremendous strain

For her brother needed surgery
Which her folks, could not afford
So her father said one day
We need a miracle, from the Lord

So she went into her closet
And removed her penny jar
She counted, one dollar twenty cents
She was very pleased by far

Then she took her jar of pennies
To the local pharmacy
She looked right up at the owner
Then she asked, "Can you help me?"

For I'd like to buy a miracle
Can you sell me one today?
See, my brother he is very ill
I have money, I can pay!

Then the druggist said to her
Child, we do not sell miracles
As the tears welled in her eyes, she said
Where else can I go?

Just then, a stranger walked over
He asked may I please help you
Can you take me to your brother
I will see what I can do

See the stranger was a surgeon
He would operate for free
And her brother he got better
With long life expectancy

And the moral of this story
It is obvious by far
We should all have faith as strong as
This child, with her penny jar

For God's miracles are waiting
And there's many blessings too
Just have faith that when you pray to him
He will always answer you.

Condemnation

You come to me, condemn someone
Then ask for my reply
You want that I, should be a judge
The judge he, lives on high

There was a time, that I'd join in
And I'd backstab away
But now I follow Jesus Christ
This is a brand new day

You have to see, that I have changed
For in the Lord there's peace
My lips they will not gossip
My condemning others ceased

When I look at another, I see now
A human being
With frailties, and problems
That lie deep and can't be seen

The only perfect being is
The Lord God, almighty
So when you feel, to put one down
Please do not come to me.

Because you trouble my spirit
When you run to me with tales
And you do these things most often
Just like clock work, never fails

I will ask you now to spare me
From your wagging vicious tongue
Or wonder why when you see me
I'm always on the run

A wicked mouth it is kin to
A most dark and wicked heart
So stop talking yourself into hell
From this habit, you must part.

Jesus Can

I know something, you don't know
Jesus is the way to go
He gives love beyond compare
He's a friend, he's always near

Give yourself to him, today
Learn his warmth
And learn his way
If you thirst, he'll hydrate you

With his spirit, tried and true
For the Lord, he is the light
Learn to do, what's just and right
Then prepare, his kingdom come

Jesus Christ, won't be undone
When the master, does return
Just like chaff
Some folks will burn

Be prepared, he's on his way
And he has a lot to say
Feed the hungry, clothe the poor
Give of yourself and much more

Do so for the least of man
You will fit, into God's plan
Quench the thirsty, help them drink
Help the lost folks on the brink

Standing at the gates of hell
You will know them, you can tell
Give a hand, do so today
Teach the children how to pray

Be a light of love and hope
Be a hand up, be a rope
For this all, your blessings flow
If you take the time to know

Jesus Christ the son of man
He will change you, Jesus can.

Arrest a Fall

The Lord has blessed us all with life
And then, he sent us out to work
Yes to glorify his holy name
In a world, that's gone beserk

Our work, it is cut out for us
The hours hard and long
We pray and praise almighty God
Then sing to him our songs

We try to thwart the enemy
And gather up the lost
We suffer persecution
We push on at any cost

Because our lord, is merciful
We give to him our best
At the end of all our toil and pain
The good lord, gives to us rest

At the end of our long journey
We will travel on back home
And the lord, he waits at heaven's gate
So we know we're not alone

And then if the lord, approves of
How we've served many and one
He will gather us into his arms
He will softly say, "Well done!"

Our rest it will be wonderful
We will enter dreamless sleep
To await the final judgment
The lord's promises, he keeps

If we've done good deeds in secret
In glory, there's treasures stored

Then the lord who knows all secrets
Will give us, our just rewards

So get out there everybody
And work for the father well
Help him fight the fight of faith
And keep your brothers out of hell.

Our Talks

You were feeling alone
So we'd talk on the phone
And we'd talk about Jesus, that day
We would talk of the scriptures

His promise, his love
Then we'd both take a moment to pray
From the depths of depression
You'd fight your way back

When reminded of our father's love
A love that will endure
You're inspired, you soar
For you fit in his arms, like a glove

With our talks at an end
And your spirits on mend
I'd confess my love then say, so long
Then I'd smile when I'd think

How you felt so unloved
And I'd tell you that
You were so wrong
I'm so glad that God used me

To speak to you, dear
And appeal to you in such a way
That you'd hang up that phone
With a smile on your face
And you would do so, that very day

Now my mother, my princess, my angel
You have been taken, away from me
I can't talk with you now, about Jesus
For you're in heaven, happy and free

And though I'll miss our
Great conversations
You live in the confines of my heart
I will look for you there

When I'm lonely and blue
And in that way, we will never part.

Unlocked

Adam and satan
The flesh and the sin
This is when the downfall
Of all men, doth begin

In the Garden of Eden
Adam he, disobeyed
And since man has been living
In sin to this day

The serpent, the women
The fruit of that tree
Brought death and damnation
To you and to me

Then all folks that followed
Were born into sin
And now folks show unrighteousness
With a grin

But God with his mercy
Sent Jesus to fight
To give up his life
Turning darkness, to light

The blood of the lamb
Made us all, white as snow
And now in this great faith
We are all free to grow

Jesus the good shepherd
The gate, and the rock
Now no longer in satan's grip
Are we all locked

Splendor

I want so, to go to heaven
That's my one and only goal
So I stay away from things
That I know, could corrupt my soul

And I keep my mind on Jesus
Who is with me, everyday
I look forward to the quiet times
When I can kneel down and pray

Folks, I love to read the scriptures
For they tell me of my home
That the lord is now preparing
In a realm where peace is sown

In the meantime I will love my God
With all my might and soul
I will spread the good news where I can
Stay on my lord's honor roll

Then one day, if I'm worthy
I will see his gentle face
He will say welcome, then hold me close
In a warm loving embrace

For my lord, is truly wonderful
And I know that he loves me
There will come a day, I will hold his hand
Every angel there to see

That day I will stand on holy ground
And walk through, those pearly gates
I will then know I've succeeded
For splendor will be my fate

No Exits

We all know, God is awesome
This is fact, this is so true
He is mighty, and he's able
There is nothing, he can't do

For he raised the dead
Gave to the blind sight
Only God saves souls
Makes our days all bright

He possesses strong undying love
He loves us the best
Heaven's pure
White dove

And his love for us
It will never change

Even when we sin, causing him
Much pain

But persistent sin
It will eat away
Chances to join Christ's
Kingdom come, some day

So folks,
I just wanted you to know
Change your ways, for
Fires down below

And this story isn't fiction
It is something I must tell
Just in case you did not know it
There are no exits, in hell

A Home in Hell

The more that I believe in God
The less, I believe man
I see right through their wretched lies
Their false pretense, and then

I take them with a grain, or salt
With everything they say
Because they do not stand for truth
No, not in any way

Some say, that I am paranoid
But I know, who speaks the truth
This person is the son of man
The Bible is the proof

For man will lead you down a path
Which always points to south
And I despise the lies and cons
That spew out of their mouths

Now in this world today, folks
There is so much treachery
Our CEO's, are stealing from
The likes of you and me

Some folks give out codes of color
To cover, protection lax
So if there should be an incident
They can cover, their own backs

They raise the taxes up so high
Some people cannot live
They say the city's strapped for cash
How much more, can we give

The subway fare is hiked
Causing the poor, much hurt and pain
Just so some greedy company
Can show tremendous gain

But folks take heart
And keep the faith
For these things, will transpire
And when the Lord returns
These thieves, he'll cast into the fire

These people do not fear God now
But soon, they will be shown
For all their lies and treachery
That hell, will be their home.

No More Fears

I feel so bad for my father
He has worked so hard, for us
He has made this world, and created man
Then he gave man, every trust

Yes he made man, and he gave to him
The dominion over all
And he loved man so, for man was his heart
But then man, would surely fall

For the enemy was lurking nigh
When I think of this, I just want to cry
The Lord God, in all his majesty
Made a perfect world, for you and me

But the serpent, reared his ugly head
He deceived the man, he was good as dead
For when Adam ate of the tree of life
He was prompted by, his adoring wife

Who had listened to the serpent's lies
Their sentence was death
They were so surprised
And ever since, that fateful day

Satan tries to take, what God gave away
He has tried with deadly sabotage
To destroy this world
And man's faith, dislodge

But he won't succeed, he will fail each time
We'll see his defeat
It will be sublime
When the sun falls down

And the Lord returns
In the great abyss, he will crash and burn
Then the Lord will rein

For a thousand years
Bringing peace at last
No more death, or fears

The Best Food

Now the table is set
Their is much food and drink
There's a welcome mat out
The host he's in the pink

He is happy and proud
That you will be his guest
And that you'll be well fed
For his food is the best

And folks, if you are thirsty
You can quench your thirst too
For his wells are abundant
And are there just for you

Then folks, after you've eaten
You'll hunger no more
You will be filled and nourished
By the one you adore

And you'll no longer thirst
For you will drink your fill
From the savior's rich fountain
And this liquid won't spill

You'll feel splendor and blissful
You will shout, with pure joy
For you've tasted the waters
And all doubts are destroyed

You will walk away filled
With the spirit of God
There will be transformation
And this change won't be hard

Every word of the Lord
You will gladly digest
In his words there is power
To this folks, I attest

Depart with Pride

Folks, heaven is my real home
I chose earth for a vacation
I have been trying for so long
Just to navigate, this station

The earth does possess all that we need
For God has made it so
We can find, all sorts of learning tools
And things to help us grow

We can find ourselves in trouble
If we don't obey the Lord
We must keep our minds on heaven
To remain safe and restored

We can learn to give and receive love
The greatest gift of all
We can learn from our mistakes
And catch ourselves, before we fall

We can learn that letting the flesh rule
Can only bring us down
We'll be wallowing in satan's filth
Right down here on this ground

We can learn that if we thirst and hunger
For God's righteousness
We can always turn to Jesus
Because our Lord, he's the best

And folks, when this trip is over
And it's time to pack our bags
We'll learn nothing will go with us
No not, diamonds, gold or rags

We will learn only to cherish
What the spirit holds inside
So this trip will not be wasted
And we can depart with pride

The Trade

Trade the good news
For the bad news, folks
Put that newspaper down
Now just go pick up that Bible

This advice is very sound
The news tells us of disaster
Mayhem, murder and disease
But the Bible tells of glory

That we can obtain, with ease
Yes the news is bad, most every day
And folks, it's getting worse
In the Bible you can find contentment

With each line and verse
Yes the news will make you troubled
And most sorry in the end
But the Bible tells of God's great love
So pick it up, my friend

And you will not want to put it down
You will find peace in great stages
But in the news, you will only learn
Of war and how it rages

Yes the Bible tells of Jesus
And his service toward man
It reminds us of eternal life
Which is very close at hand

The Bible gives us hope and tells
Us Jesus will return
The news tells us, of wild fires
And how intense, they burn

Yes in the Bible you will find
Encouragement and truth
While the media, will tell us of
Our lost and troubled youth

Yes folks, do pick up the Bible
It is the best text to choose
Now put down that old newspaper
Read the Bible, it's good news

Forget Me Not

Will you still be my mom and my love
When I see you in heaven, above?
Will you love me like you, used to do
Even though we're in bodies anew?

Will you recognize me just the same?
Will you even remember my name?
I am wondering how it all will be
When you first lay your eyes, upon me

So much time has elapsed, since you've gone
And the emptiness pricks, like a thorn
But in Jesus I will come your way
I cannot wait for that wondrous day

How I long to be held, in your arms
To revisit your warmth and your charm
I cannot forget your warm embrace
Will I still be yours, when we are in grace?

Will the love that we shared on the earth
Be the same way upon heaven's turf?
I am praying hard this will all be so
From my earthly mom, I just want to know

These are questions, that tug at my heart
They began with your need to depart
I am praying you will not forget

While you take your sweet eternal rest
Then I'll know love remains in your heart
And from that sweet love I will never part.

The Quenching

Drops of water, from a faucet
Water rushing from a falls
Liquid diamonds from a fountain
Nourishing the thirsts of all

Raging waters in a river
Giant waves crest with the tides
Roaring glistening in the sunlight
On a surf board, some folks ride

So refreshing and hydrating
Bathe in it or drink your fill
Satisfaction—will be short lived
They'll remain a thirst there still

If your thirst cannot be quenched and
Earthly springs and streams won't do
Turn to Jesus, he's the answer
With the word, he'll hydrate you

Drink of him absorb his essence
And I promise you my friend
There will be applause in glory
And you'll never thirst again

Jesus is the living waters
Come wade in his loving flow
He will permeate your spirit
And your faith and trust will grow

What a cleansing quenching savior
For his springs will never ebb
He's the gate, he's the redeemer
Be entwined in heaven's web

What Sin?

Then I eased out of the darkness
And I stepped—into the light
That's where Jesus Christ was waiting
He stood there, just to my right

Then I ran into his open arms
And we both stood there and we cried
He said, "I'm so glad you've come
Before both soul and spirit died."

Then I begged, O please Lord forgive me
As the tears streamed down my face
I have sinned and shamed my father
And to him, I'm a disgrace

Then the Lord asked me a question
That would stir my soul within
And I knew I was forgiven
When the Lord asked me, "What sin?"

The next thing I knew, I was but
An infant in his arms
The Lord carried me a long ways
He held me through every storm

And he taught to me the scriptures
Right on through my toddler stage
He helped me to grow in righteousness
In my teachings to engage

Now he keeps up at a normal pace
For I'm walking right behind
I am staying on this lighted path
I won't ever change my mind

For me sin is not an option
Nor is suffering and pain
I have found love ever lasting
I will never sin again.

The Godly Way

Our God loves a cheerful giver
So let's give without restraint
With an open mind and an open heart
Loving pictures we must paint

We will give our gifts in secret
And we'll never brag or boast
About the good things, that we have done
For the ones who need the most

And then God, who knows all secrets
Will give to us our just due
With stored blessings up in heaven
Kept there safely just for you

There are some who seek approval
From those who are earthly bound
And they brag about, each act or deed
Yes to everyone around

See this short-lived recognition
Is all that they will receive
They'll be no praises in glory
This fete they will not achieve

So, be humbled and be gracious
When you give, give with a smile
Be sincere with your intentions
Be as trusting as a child

Then the heavens will smile on you
You will be blessed every day
So folks, let us give to those who need
For it is, the godly way.

Finality

Your heart has stopped beating
Your eyes are now closed
Your mouth, does not utter
You will be in repose

The spirit and soul, that's
Propelled you for years
Has left now, and gone home
Everyone is in tears

There is stillness, and silence
And there's mystery there
What's become of you?
Should I rejoice, or have fear?

Our loving and touching
Has now come to a halt
If you'd just speak to me
I would do somersaults

Devastation, frustration
Are with me each day
For the angels, have taken
My mother away

Some folks say "Don't you worry!"
"She's in a good place!"
And I know this because of my
Lord's love and grace.

But the pain and the memories
Will tear at my heart
Because all of a sudden
You and I had to part

It's so final, disruptive
My whole life, has been changed
Now I must live without you
It is lonely . . . and strange

Without a Trace

Well beyond life, as we know it
Therein lies, another place
It's a place where there is no more time
And no measurement of space

Living folks, will never know of
Any secrets, this place holds
And the deceased, they will never share
For they all, have other goals

Yes for eons, man has questioned
Where the dear departed go
They scrutinize and summarize
And they agonize so

There are men who make up stories
While some others, fantasize
But on this subject, man will not know
Yes no matter how he tries

There has never been a returnee
So we'll never know first hand
Just what happens when we pass
To that obscure and distant land

Foolish man, can split the atom
He can now visit the stars
But he'll never know God's secrets
He will never get that far

So folks, if you're interested
You can get into this act
You will need a one way ticket
And you will not have to pack

You came into this world naked
And that's how your gonna leave
You must say farewell to every friend
And your family, will grieve.

Then you walk into obscurity
Where all memory is erased
Tell them don't bother to search for you
You'll be gone without a trace

Higher Learning

I want to be a graduate
In the school of, higher learning
So I'm making very sure
Heavenly merits, I am earning

I am studying the Bible
And revealing all I know
So that when the time comes for the test
I will pass and I will grow

I'll be well informed in godly love
So folks, then scholastically
I will excel in this righteous course
And my grades will exalt me

I will be well schooled in mercy
I will keep my grades up high
For the time when I'll matriculate
To that classroom, in the sky

Then the angels will take over
Prepare me for my new job
For the holy degree I'll receive
Will be given out by God

I will then be a professional
In the ways of my sweet Lord
I'll reside in the Lord's mansion
For he's welcomed me aboard

I will teach every newcomer
To this wondrous realm of love
We will live in peace and splendor
With our savior up above.

Call His Name

I work for God almighty
I am in his employ
I bring to every one I meet
His words of hope and joy

I tell them to depend on God
To trust him, for he's able
To ask in faith, and they'll receive
He is constant, loving, stable

I am filled with information
That I feel I must reveal
That Jesus is alive and well
And heaven it is real

I must tell about the blood of Christ
Which has cleansed our minds and souls
And about a love constant and true
That won't cease and won't grow cold

I must tell all, that the time is nigh
For Jesus to return
They must all repent, for time is short
If they don't they'll surely burn

I must tell them that in Jesus Christ
There's life that will not end
I will tell them he's our savior
And he's also a good friend

I'll inform them that, to speak with God
They must first go through his son
Jesus Christ interprets every prayer
Yes folks, Jesus is the one

I must tell them where they all can find
Freedom from all sin and shame
They must put their earthly cares aside
And then call on the Lord's name

The Lord's Work

Refurbishing, rewarding
Refreshing, renewing
Is what my Lord Jesus is
Constantly doing

Encouraging, saving, uplifting
Redeeming
He cleanses our souls
Sets our spirits to beaming

He's feeding the hungry
And those who would thirst
With the true word of God
In great bounds and great bursts

He's armed with faith, honesty
Honor and truth
He is good to the weak
And he protects the youth

He is healing revealing consoling
Controlling the faint and the frail
For all saints he's enrolling

He is sighing he's crying he mourns
For the dying
He is pushing forgiveness
And constantly trying

He is beautiful, wondrous, king of all kings
He is master of this world
Ruler of all things

He's the giver of light
And he knows every heart
From his glory and spirit
We shall never part

Her Change

God has changed her mortal soul
Going to heaven is her goal
Before she chose these gifts so well
She was headed straight to hell

She drank and smoked and swore and then
She went to bed, with many men
Searching for love with any stranger
Putting her soul, in mortal danger

Now she is cleansed, she did repent
For being saved, is heaven sent
This girl was blind, devoid of sight
But the Lord came to her, one night

He told her, that she'd truly die
If she continued to defy
She must start now, to throw off sin
Or she could never, live with him

He told her of a dismal place
Where there's no love or light
And then her eyes began to see
And what an awesome sight

The Lord he stood before her
With his arms stretched out to hold
And when she stepped into his arms
She was no longer cold

And now she's changed
She's trying hard
To be what the Lord wants
This girl, no longer, frequents bars

Or other sinful haunts
And this girl prays
Most every day
She praises God for grace

She knows one day she will
Reside
In God's most holy place.

The Lord's Paradise

I am here, but I'm not
For my heart, it is broken
You can tell by my smile
Not a word, need be spoken

See, my beautiful mother
Has been taken away
And I can't stop my tears
I am sad, every day

Although I know that she
Is with God, and at peace
I feel it will take years
For my sorrows to cease

I miss her oh so much
I hear her favorite songs
Even though she has not been
Away very long

I am not sleeping well, I awake easily
Then I pray that my mom
Would be there next to me
Just a whisper or phrase

From her would compensate
For the fact, she has gone
Through heaven's pearly gate
But the Lord, he is good

He will heal me someday
He will mend my poor heart
For it's to him I pray
He'll remind me that in faith

No one really dies
He will comfort me between
My sobbing and sighs
Then he'll give me the strength

And the will to go on
He'll erase all my grief
He will mend, what is torn

I will listen to him
I will take his advice
That I'll see her one day
In the Lord's paradise

There my joy will return
And my spirits will soar
I'll run into her arms
I won't ever need more

Unimportant Things

Earthly treasures cannot go
With me to heaven
And I won't be needing them
When I go there

For I've built up treasures
In my father's kingdom
And I won't have any room
For them to spare

Earthly pain and heartache
Aren't welcomed either
For it is a place of purity and grace
There are oh so many wondrous things awaiting

And a big angelic smile
On every face
This is why we never take anything with us
What belongs to earth

Will always stay behind
For in heaven there are treasures
Unimagined
And folks every one of them
A glorious find

So don't take to heart
These earthly things you've gathered
For they never are important, in the end
Neither status neither title, nor ambition

Will exalt your soul
So on them don't depend
No folks, it is not your flesh
Or your possessions

That will save you and redeem you
No my friends
How you spread the Lord God's glory
Is what matters
Never what you own,
And these rules do not bend

Someone Sees

When you're alone
Do you feel that
No one sees what you do?
If you steal or lie or cheat

There is no one, who's watching you?
Do you feel that what you're doing
It will never be revealed?
Well hate to burst your bubble, friend

But the Lord sees, that's the deal
There is nothing you may do or say
That the Lord won't know about
And he can hear what you're saying

In a whisper or a shout
You don't have to say a word, for the Lord
Knows what's in your heart
You cannot hide from the master

I'd advise you not to start
He knows everything about you
Down to the smallest detail
If you ride the train of satan

Know that you will be derailed
There's no secrets from, almighty God
You're a fool, if you think so
If you swim unrighteous waters

You will feel God's undertow
So folks please don't try to hide
For our God, he's always aware
If you want to go to hell

Know sin, will always take you there
So please trust me when I tell you
You're exposed every day
Now wise up, and live in righteousness
For it is the only way.

Don't Cry
(A Message From God)

Why do you cry?
You must be of good cheer
For you know that your mother
Is with me, I'm here

I have introduced her to
The angels above
She is now busy greeting
The one's that she loves

She will never be lonely
She'll ever have pain
She won't ever have problems
Or heartaches again

She is now dressed in white robes
That are trimmed with gold
She is young and vibrant
She will never grow old

She resides in a mansion
Which I have prepared
With her family there
All my glory is shared

So do not cry for her
She believed and she's saved
She now has a new body
And her soul, has been raised

Now rejoice in the Lord
He is just he is fair
He has taken your mom
With the utmost of care

And if you now believe
On the Lord, Jesus Christ
You will see her again
When you reach, paradise

Please be brave and be strong
She would want it that way
Live a good and just life
And remember to pray

Grateful

I'm grateful that—you stand by me
When times are hard
And I can't see
My way out of—trouble and doubt

I'm glad you're there
To help me out
No matter what—I know you're near
Through every anguish—every fear

You hold me close—each time I call
You lift me up—you are my all
The hardest thing—for one to take
Is when a relative—forsakes

But you won't change
And you don't lie
I love you so—and this is why
My Lord you are—more than a friend

Your love is real—you don't pretend
So when my friends—turn against me
You save me Lord—then set me free

These words are merely—human words
They may sound childish—or absurd
Lord it's the only—way I know
To tell you that—I love you so

With you my strength—is at its peak
I cannot fail—I'm never weak
So Lord I thank you
Gratefully

For being there
For being thee

In My Dreams

I know you're a breath,
Just a whisper away
Like an unexplored dream
Or an unrealized day

Like a smoke or a mist
Swirling round in the dawn
You were here for a while
Now you're suddenly gone

There is no fantasy
There's no music or band
And the only thing left
Is for what, a life stands

It is simple and silent
No mystery at all
Just requires a heart
That is stilled, or has stalled

It requires a God
Who is just and is fair
That will take back his spirit
When it is in despair

It requires a love,
That is ageless and true
And a God ever present
So he can, redeem you

It requires a soul
That will be put to rest
It requires a life
That's done its very best

Then memories and pictures
They come into play
And there are broken hearts
That cry tears every day

But the essence and love
Will remain just as long
As a favorite expression
Or the words of a song

A dimension is all
A membrane or a wall
Just a very sheer curtain
Just a slip, not a fall

So my love you are here
It's not bad as it seems
I look forward, to seeing your smile
In my dreams.

Without God

She got pregnant, they were married
They broke up, in just two years
Now she sits there, with her children
She's impoverished, and in tears

Her small children, look up to her
For protection, and for love
These small children, they are gifts
From God, they're sent from up above

She gets lonely for a lover
And she finds herself a man
She does everything to keep him
She does everything, she can

In the mean time, her small babies
Are neglected and alone
For she really has, no interest
In making, a happy home

They grow up, and they are angry
They have little, self-esteem
To their children, they're neglectful
They are downright, harsh and mean

For you see folks, there's a cycle
When we do things, without God
We do suffer, needless torturers
And we make our lives, so hard

So young folks, please think
Before you act, ask God to intervene
He will guide you, and stand by you
He'll be there, though, he's not seen

He will always keep you safe and
Give you judgment, that is sure
For his love it, is eternal
And no one could, ask for more

Scientific

Man says the world was made
From big explosions, long ago
And in a cave, the first man he did dwell
Man says the moon and stars
Were made for scientific reasons

Man has us on a pathway, straight to hell
On scientific programs man
Explains the whole creation
And what they say, does not include our God

The one who turned a formless void
Into the earth we live on
The one who gave it life
Which he enjoyed

The one who worked hard for six days
Then took a blessed break
On the seventh day he rested
For there was no more at stake

You see, God created man himself
And gave him great dominion
So folks, take it with a grain of salt
These men and their opinions

Because science does not speak of God
In any publications
And they don't admit the fact that
Only God can create nations

The Bible says, that God himself
Made mountains, stars and trees
He planted every blade of grass
Created birds and bees

In the Bible there are truth in words
Right out of God's own mouth
So folks, read the Bible find the truth
Or join man, who's going south

Until My Dying Day

Through all my wild and wicked days
You've never left my side
You begged me to come home with you
But I'd turn run, and hide

For I felt if I went with you
Then my fun, it would be over
So I stayed away, I ran and hid
I used the dark for cover

So in love with useless habits
That I often would repeat
Is the reason why, when my Lord spoke
I'd cower and retreat.

I was stubborn and remorseless
Filled with pride and filled with rage
I did not have time for praying
My folly had come of age

But your mercies, they are endless
When I fell, you picked me up
You forgave when I repented
Then my God, you filled my cup

Now the fun, I thought that I would miss
Seems distant and seems trite
I have now a clean clear conscience
And I'm sleeping well at night

I have you my Lord to thank for
Guiding me gently away
I will pray and praise forever
Yes until my dying day.

They Must Turn

There are people groping in the dark
As blind as they can be
When they are called, these folks won't hear
This often puzzles me

Why won't they heed, the call of God?
Why won't they stop and think?
For don't they know their lives
Can end as fast as they can blink

And what will they say to the Lord
How will they all explain
Why they chose fun and folly
And they lived their lives in vain

Lord I am trying very hard
To open up their eyes
Because if they will not change
They'll all get a big surprise

The mouth of hell is open wide
So they'll be swallowed up
For they're playing now with fire
And they all are so corrupt

Help me God to say the right words
Please assist me while I try
For they know not what their doing
And for sin, they'll surely die

Help me Lord, to be successful
Help me to turn them around
Or they'll live in satan's chambers
For forever, how profound.

Directions for Salvation

First get down on your knees
And confess all your sins
And then go get baptized
So you'll be born again

Read the Bible each day
From beginning to the end
It will give you the answers
To all questions, my friend

Stay in touch with Christ Jesus
While awake and asleep
So that each of his promise
To you he'll keep

Pray and praise God almighty
Whether glad or when sad
And when troubles assail you
Then you won't feel so bad

You must always do good
For whom ever you can
And for righteousness and truth
You must always stand

When you show God you're trusting
And that you avoid sin
You may now establish
A relation, with him

If you stay on this course
And you don't turn around
You will find that God's love
Is the best to be found

Then your life it will change
For the better you see
He will do this for you
He has done this for me

Praise the Lord God Almighty
For in him we are saved
And his mercy and love
On our hearts is engraved

There is triumph in him
There is victory too
Come now, folks get on board
Come and live life anew

Alzheimer's

He does not know, what he's doing
He does not know that he's loud
For this man he has Alzheimer's
Of this I'm sure he's not proud

He's confused with fear of falling
Feels he's falling while he sits
Wheels his chair around in circles
He's at the end of his wits

While he's here we must protect him
Show him God's graces and love
God gave charge over these people
He watches us from above

Show compassion while he's yelling
Speak to him in gentle tones
And don't ever lose your temper
Never make him feel alone

Precious soul in your confusion
Know that we are here for you
We will show you love and mercy
Be encouraging and true

We could be in your position
But for God's graces we go
We'll behave like God's brave soldiers
Grace and mercy we will sow

An Angry Child

She walked away
From me that day
So angry and so proud
The last words, that she spoke to me

Were filled with rage, and loud
But I did nothing to her
To stir this wretched ire
And she seemed out of character

Stuck in anger's muck and mire
Then she called and left a message
That I won't see her again
And my heart was truly broken

But now it is on the mend
For I kept in touch with Jesus
And he won't leave me alone
Now my pain is slowly ebbing

As I pray for her atone
You see folks, I love my daughter
She's the only one I have
She has lost her faith and courage

And she's made me feel so bad
But I pray for her soul often
I ask God to help her back
Into his arms and protection

And to put her, back on tract
In the meantime, I will miss her
She'll be always on my mind
I pray she will regain her sight

So she'll no longer be blind
My dear sweet Lord, my shield my rock
Please bring my child, back to the flock
And make her days, all bright again

And let her know, You're her best friend

The Opposition

There is nothing you could say, to me
That I'd ever want to hear
So don't try your flattery again
Thinking to me, you'll get near

For I oppose your gross ideas
And I do, detest your ways
I know well that I will feel this way
Throughout all my living days

I'm aware, that over centuries
You've aimed to destroy, mankind
With temptations, lies and cunning
You search out the weak and blind

You spread hate disease and sorrow
Yes, wherever you may go
You encourage immorality
And deceit is what you sow

I am wise to all your wicked ways
I will warn all that I can
Up until the time, the Lord returns
Dragging you away from man

He will cast you and your helpers
Down into the pit of hell
Never to return, you will surely burn
Where all satan's minims dwell

For you represent destruction
And you represent what's vile
You have tripped up God's folks long enough
We rebuke you, with a smile

Half-Stepping

If you just dip, your toe in the water
Then you can't say
that you've had a bath
If you walk down a road
When you travel

Then you can't say, you've
Taken the path
If a man shaves one half of
The hair on his face
Then he can't say, that he has been shaved

If you only paddle on your surfboard
Then you can't say, that you caught a wave

By the same token, being a Christian
My friends—you really are, or you're not
For you can't be luke warm
With your passion for God

You are either cold, or you are hot
I know some folks that say
They have God in their hearts
If you heard them speak
You wouldn't know

They're immoral, and cunning
They backstab away
And they act like they care
Just for show

You can't half step with God
You can't do it!
I say that you can't have it
Both ways

You can't work for the Lord, and the devil
If you think so, you've shortened your days
I am sayin to you, it is urgent
That you make up your minds
Right away

For the devil, is waiting
To possess your soul
And the Lord will be here
Any day

So don't say to me, that
You just dabble
In religion, because your
Not sure

You can be very sure
That the devil is real
And he wants your soul
And much much more

Now, get down on your knees
be repentant
Ask forgiveness before it's too late
Get the Lord on your side
There is no place to hide

Or the dark cold abyss
Be your fate.

The Double-Edged Sword

You are now, comfortably riding
On the double sword of hell
You commit adultery, and you fornicate
I'd advise you to, stand up right now

And walk, away from darkness
And my friend,
Please do so before it's too late
What will you say to the Lord
When your life on earth is through

How on earth will you explain
The path you took
If you think that you're in love
Or have fears of being alone
I'd advise you now, to take a second look

There is no pleasure or action
That is worth your mortal soul
Which if you stay on this path
You'll surely lose

The Lord God is merciful
But he won't ever force his way
So he gave us the ability to choose
There is still time, my good friend

You can get another chance
For as long as there is life
There's always hope
So stop hiding in the shadows

Take a stand, give God your heart
Have some courage, and backbone
Don't be a dope
For the body dies and rots away

It betrays us in the end
So don't let the flesh have power over you
You will thank the stars you did
For from satan you'll be rid
And the Lord God,
To you always will be true

Christ Tabernacle
(*My Church*)

My soul cries out, my spirits soar
The moment I, walk through its doors
I feel refreshed, I'm not alone
I feel that I, have just come home

Inside there's one big family
With smiles and warmth, they welcome me
I feel God's spirit in the air
And I just know, that Christ is there

There's Pastor Durso, he's the best
He leads his flock, through all life's tests
There's Pastor Carey, with the choir
His music the masses, admire
He touches all spiritually
With every gospel melody

The elders, touched by the divine
They make me feel, that all is mine
And once I'm there, it's hard to leave
The service ends, I feel to grieve

I do pay tithes, but don't belong
I sing a sad, and lonely song
Now my heart feels, compelled to join
To find a pocket, for this coin

I won't be outside, looking in
I'll find a worth and joy, within
Until the day, my Lord returns
I'll serve his church, and then I'll earn

God's holy merits as I do
It's now my pleasure
To join you.

Life

We arrive when it's time
And we leave, when it's time
Because our lives, they are not our own
We are here for one reason

That is to repay, every glory
Our father has shown
Like a leaf in the water
Propelled by the wind

We are moved by, God's mighty right hand
Our direction unseen
Like a leaf in a stream
Our life's journey, is all in God's plan

Life beings with fanfare
And it ends, in despair
Hearts are broken
And tears won't abate

We are blessed to be born
The next moment, we're gone
This is what our life holds
It's our fate

So do not say that you
Plan to do this or that
In the next day, the next month or year
You had better confer

With your father above
To repel, disappointment and tears
For the Lord will give answers
Direction and love

If we'll only consult him in prayer
So be wise call on him
He will answer you soon
And have faith, that the Lord God will hear

Only fools do their planning
Without God's permission
And they all come up short, every time

So acknowledge your Lord
Doing so, brings rewards
And a life on this earth
That's sublime.

The Undoing

He is deadly, and he's cunning
He has always defied God
He would undo all that God has done
With his lies and his facades

He is lurking in the shadows
For some unsuspecting soul
He has in mind your destruction
Your damnation is his goal

Yes he makes sin, seem attractive
He loves immorality
He is putrid, scum, filth and disease
With his sights, on you and me

He has legions, he has minions
To do all his bidding and
I am speaking of the devil
He and death go hand and hand

God has done so much for mankind
Since he placed mankind on earth
We must fight the hand of darkness
We must never give lust birth

We must join the army of the Lord
Put the armor of God on
We must keep our eyes on heaven
We must be faithful and strong

For the Lord God will protect us
And with him we cannot fail
We must fast and pray, and praise all day
And to paradise, we'll sail

The Path

He was happy and smiling as
He walked God's trail
With the sun and the wind on his face
And God' plan was revealing itself
To him there

If he'd follow, he'd do so in grace
As he traveled he noticed, a beautiful girl
She would beckon to him as he walked
She said, "Step off the trail for a moment
In time.

So that we two could have a nice talk!"
And it seemed to this boy
That he traveled alone
At the time he did not know the word

So that when the Lord warned this boy
to stay the course
The Lord's warnings, they were never heard
Now this young man stepped off

Of this well lighted path
And he ran to the beautiful girl
Never knowing that satan had fooled him again
And his actions would ruin his world

For this women, he lied and he cheated and stole
Placing him in a jail, for some time
And the people in charge
They would not forgive him

For they said he'd committed a crime
So the young man, he picked up the Bible one day
And he asked the Lord, please to forgive
For the darkness of sin, it has surrounded him
And he felt, he could no longer live

God forgave him of course
Told the boy to have faith
And be sure his deliverance is nigh
And since God has the last word in all circumstance
He would give his answer, by and by

I don't know of the end of this story
But I'm sure God will always come through
And the moral to this
If by grace you were kissed

Never stray from the path
I warn you.

Never Missed

Folks, it isn't Mother Nature
But the Lord God in his wrath
For he wants your full attention
You must walk, a righteous path

So he sends to us disasters
Fires, earthquakes, and tornados
For we wallow deep in sin
And every heart only the Lord knows

On that day of nine eleven
Sounds of death, were very loud
The Lord God, he did allow this
For those people, were too proud

There was sexual perversion
Child abuse, murder and rape
Much corruption and injustice
They were all in such bad shape

New York City, God's creation
Is now Sodom and Gomorrah
They're immoral, they are wicked
Even folks who read the Torah

They divide their population
By their color race or creed
They don't look out for their people
Who are homeless or in need

Satan, he has taken over
There is not a righteous one
Who loves justice faith and honor
Who respects, God's only son

Know the Lord's time, it is nearing
And he is soon to return
Then the judgment will begin
And most folks, will just crash and burn

Then the prince of air, the devil
Will cast into the abyss
For a thousand years, he'll stay there
Ever hated, never missed

Take Heed

Child, heed the words
Of those who know
Don't make the same mistakes
For just one trip on satan's snares

Is all that it will take
To turn your future upside down
Leaving you broke and sad
You don't know how bad it can be

If by satan, you're had
Don't close your eyes and close your mind
And say, "I'm above all,"
"I will not do, what you have done!"

This will be your downfall
Child, keep your young mind open
And do not let the flesh rule
If you yield to this temptation

You will wind up being fooled
You see, satan wants to destroy
Every young and budding life
If you take, what he will offer

It will lead to pain and strife
Child, I'm speaking from experience
I have been up, to bat
I can tell you, right this moment

That I've been there, and done that
If you'll only heed the wisdom
Of the elders you will see
That you won't wind up, with broken dreams

As has, the likes of me

The Devil's Trap

The devil, he has tripped you up
Just like I said he would
He tempted you, you took the bait
And for his wrongs, you stood

He blinded you and made you deaf
To all things that were right
He tricked you and he lied to you
He took away your light

And now you're sitting, in that jail
Asking what have I done
For satan made you feel that
You were only having fun

Now satan is hysterical
He's laughing and he's singing
Because he found another fool
The bells in hell, are ringing

But as you know, the Lord
Is filled with mercy and compassion
And he would never leave you
Not in any form or fashion

So ask the Lord's forgiveness
With an open sincere heart
Then make sure, you forgive yourself
Let healing get its start

You must now rebuke the devil
Send him packing, right away
Never let him hang around you
No not for, another day

We all have made mistakes in life
From yours I pray, you've learned
That when you play with satan
You will always end up burned.

Forewarned

You have been warned
You have been shown
So now, what will it be
Will you follow Christ, our savior

So your soul can now be free
Because time is running out, my friends
And the Lord, is on his way
He may show up, at just any time

Or arrive on any day
For my sisters and my brothers
The Lord's time, is getting nigh
You can't half step with Christ Jesus

And for you, the stakes are high
For the devil and his minions
They are searching for lost souls
To destroy mankind, in anyway

It is satan's only goal
See there is a battle raging
It is fierce, and it is strong
In the spirit world, and outer realms

There's a fight for right and wrong
Where the angels battle darkness
Armed with righteousness and truth
They are fighting hard, and fighting long

With the might and strength of youth
Now it's time to choose
No more time to play
You are in or you are out

Please heed what I say
It may be today
That you hear, the angels shout

Rebuke the Sin

I am just there—until I'm not

So things don't—bother
Me a lot

Yes, I was born—one day I'll die
And my life it—was never pie
I am not sure—of many things
And much regret—this sometimes brings

What I'm sure of—is the sweet fact
That the good Lord—has got my back
It's as simple—as it can be
That my father—he does love me

And I am sure—that when I pray
The good Lord hears each word I say
I am real sure—he answers prayer
I call on him—and he is there

And I am positive—you see
That the Lord he—stays close to me
I'm also sure—and it's been shown
That he will not—leave me alone

So although I—do not know much
With the Lord God—I keep in touch
For the sweet Lord—to me is all
With him I'm sure—I will not fall

You too can be—sure of his love
Serenity—from up above
Just learn to know—and love the Lord
Throw off your sins—then climb aboard

Decide

The time has come, to make a choice
You've dabbled, long enough
The fires of hell, are bearing down
The going will get tough

How can I impress, upon you
That time, is getting short
You're so consumed, with earthly woes
Though worries, come to naught

I see you and I ask you
All about your Christian walk
I ask how far you've gotten
And you give me idol talk

From what you say I know
That satan has a grip on you
For you're depressed and troubled
And you're always feeling blue

Now my good friend, I must appeal
To you in Jesus' Name
Rebuke the demons in your life
And throw away, the shame

For Jesus was torched and slain
To take away your sins
And by his stripes, we all are healed
It's time, you must begin

To throw away your worries
Every trouble, and your pain
With all of you, accept the Lord
With Christ, you'll always gain.

So do not walk away from God
Or make up some excuse
The consequence of sin is death
And eternal abuse.

The Sermon

The pastor said, it won't be easy
Trying to win over lost souls
For we fight demonic forces
Man's destruction, is their goal

He said take an armor bearer
With us when we are engaged
With the enemy, the devil
To fight his lies and his rage

Our pastor said to trust in God
For we fight the fight of faith
We must be strong, we must be bold
We must have strength, to be top rate

We are soldiers in God's army
We must save all that we can
We can't stand by and say nothing
And watch hell swallow each man

For we all represent God and
We're his eyes, his ears, his sword
This fight may get down and dirty
But we're fighting for the Lord

Can't be idle, won't be silenced
Won't be bound and we won't fear
For God marches up ahead with
Holy armor, righteous gear

We must fight hard, we must fight long
For the enemy is strong
Because evil won't relent
And some folks, they just won't repent

We have been called
The time is nigh
And we will fight
Till hell runs dry

The Party

There's a beam of light
Coming down from the Lord
And this light is so bright
That it can't be ignored

There's a melody sweet
That is filling the air
There are angels singing
And their tune, can't compare

There are trumpets, ablowing
And shouts of great joy
It's so loud the earth trembles
To this God-given ploy

And the wicked, they are running
Searching for, somewhere to hide
For they lived life, with contempt for God
And his words, they did despise

There is fire in the heavens
And the evil shake with fear
For they know they have to answer
For their sinful, shameful years

And the weak and frail
Are standing tall
They are now amongst the proud
For they hear the voice of God himself

And it is so clear, so loud
Then the judgment it, has just begun
Every one must take a turn
Because every sinner on this earth

Will be cast in fire to burn
Then the righteous will have peace and bliss
Yes for all eternity
Living in God's holy mansion

And I pray, this includes me

The Blemish

We know in the tribulation
There will be a mark required
You must have this mark to eat and drink
Or to find work, and get hired

This mark it is of the devil
Is this mark right now on you?
Could this mark of your damnation
Be your beautiful tattoo?

I see them all over people
Folks accept this mark, each day
They consider this a fashion
But they may be satan's prey

For the devil opens tattoo stores
To the prideful, weak and weary
They unwittingly get themselves tagged
Now don't let your eyes, get teary

If the good Lord wanted
You marked up
He'd have done the job, himself
Now you run to tattoo parlors
And get marked by satan's elf

I don't know for sure, this is
The mark the Bible speaks about
But folks rest assured it just may be
What will single you out

I am not trying to frighten
But I want to make you think
If this is the devil's stamp
Then you'll be finished in a wink

If you don't have one, don't get one
If you do, get it removed
It may be about, your mortal soul
Go now, get your self improved

Take a Stand

When Moses came down
From Mt. Sinai
His face shone, as bright as the sun
And the people could not
Look upon him

But they all knew that he, was the one
Who was chosen by God, to assist them
So that they could reach
The promised land

He was changed when he climbed
Down that mountain
With the tablets of God
In his hands

By the same token, every believer
Who assists the Lord God in his works
Will be changed, just as Moses forever
And they will receive, heavenly perks

I assure you, these changes transpire
At the moment you kneel and repent
So get started on the road to heaven
Your repentance will be, time well spent

Just as Moses God servant lead people
God may choose you, to do just the same
You may have to bring, every sheep back to the fold
Rescue them all from sin, wrong and shame

So remember when you serve
That you will be changed
The change in you will go hand and hand

So start serving the Lord
With your heart and your might
Against evil we must take a stand

Immorality

There are many who embrace
The wrong, abnormal and perverse
And they disregard the Bible
Yes they ignore every verse

For the Bible is against all forms
Of immorality
And folks, sexual perversion
Is the devil's prodigy

In the Bible God created man
And saw that he was lonely
So the lord created women
Yes he chose a female only

For a man and women naturally
Could populate the earth
This was all planned in God's wondrous scheme
When he gave to this world birth

Now, the devil had a hand in changing
What God made with game
For he told his folks, it was okay
To lay down with the same

And today these acts are recognized
As acts of normalcy
They have children and get married
Thus, confusing you and me

Folks, these acts of sheer perversion
In God's eyes are a disgrace
This is just one of the reasons
For ending the human race

When all wrongs are made to seem right
Then injustice will prevail
But these sinners will be, locked out
And they'll perish, without fail

God's Right

God almighty made this world
With all that it contains
He's the greatest world creator
He's the boss he is the brains

With his ageless love and knowledge
He creates, the divine plan
And then with infinite wisdom
He made woman, from a man

For a woman can bring forth new life
A woman can conceive
So the Lord made, Eve and Adam
Never was, Adam and Steve

There has not been one child reproduced
Through rectal intercourse
These ideas come straight from satan
Desperate actions, of the lost

Some people say, "Leave them alone!"
"Let them all live as they please!"
And some politicians, need their votes
So these folks, they appease

Have they ever read the Bible?
If they did, then they would see
That the Lord God, will not tolerate
Such immorality.

There are consequences to the sin
One day they will know God's wrath
Perverse acts beget disease and pain
And there's death in every path

Give in to the flesh, when satan makes
It crave for its same gender
Will get you rewards, only in hell
Right along with your defenders

For the wages of all sin is death
Open up your eyes and see
Or your soul will rot, in satan's pit
Yes for all eternity.

God Chose You

From under your breast mom
And next to your heart
I lay in your womb
Where my life, it did start

The sound of your breathing
Is what I loved best
It calmed me and gave me
Incredible rest

Through you I was nurtured
And able to grow
The bigger my size, all
The more you did show

I loved you right then dear
'Twas you I adored
It was only the good Lord
That I could love more

For the Lord, he placed me
On your warm bed of life
Then he stayed close to me
Keeping me free from strife.

And then, when my nine months of
Gestation was through
I lay in your warm arms
And I looked up at you

I knew then, that your love for
Me was very strong
You would care for and be there
For me, my life long

I am grateful and honored
For there could be no other
I was blessed by the Lord
He made you my sweet mother

My New Agent

Folks, the Lord will be my agent
And I have no more to say
For my God he will, promote the book
Titled, *Don't Forget to Pray*.

See, I wrote to many publishers
Who refused to view my work
Then I asked the Lord to intervene
And he gave me many perks

For with God, all things are possible
There is nothing, he can't do
So he gave me funds, to publish myself
Now the book is soon to view

This is one of many miracles
That my Lord has blessed me with
For he sat me down and showed me
I had many wondrous gifts

And until the day, I am dead and gone
I will write God's poetry
To encourage and enlighten
And to help set his souls free

Lord I'm happy and I'm grateful
For your love, your grace, your all
I will try my best to make you proud
Now I feel I'm ten feet tall

With your faith and help
I will publish books
To encourage and inspire
Made to change the path

Of the yet unsure
And to take them all much higher

I Don't Know You

Mayday, Mayday, going down
These are the cries
Of those who drown
Into the sea, of sinfulness

And unrepentant's hornet's nest
For these folks love
To kill and maim
They lie and cheat, their way to fame

They are a moral, and corrupt
They've fallen down and
Won't get up
The Lord called to them, many times

But they are deaf, and they are blind
They do not want, to know the Lord
They say religion, makes them bored
When they see hell, they'll turn and run

They won't think much, of having fun
They'll beg the Lord
To start anew
Then God will say, I don't know you

And they will pay
And pay dearly
Their souls, will rot in hell
You see

Folks, do not let the devil tempt
For from this fate
You're not exempt

You can sin, but only for so long
Stay close to God
He'll keep you strong.

A Victor's Song
(*A Nurse's Tale*)

My melting heart went out to him
As he sat slumped in his, wheelchair
So pale and weak, and so withdrawn
He looked so trapped in dark despair

He knew that soon, he'd have to leave
But did not want to go
For he was ravished, by disease
Yet God, still loved him so

So every chance, that I would get
In my exhausting, day
I'd take time out, to hold him close
And hug his fears, away

Because I knew the fear he had
Was fear of the unknown
I told him many, many times
That he, was not alone

For he's at the beginning of a long
And loving kiss
Yes, he will step, into a world
Of splendor and of bliss

In Jesus, there's eternal life
In Christ, no soul will die
So I told him, he must be strong
Between his sobs, and cries.

For, when we slip away from this life
It is not the end
It's the beginning of new things
Believe what I say, friend

And when it's time for all of us
To fall, into that sleep
We can be sure, that God almighty
Has our souls, to keep

The next time we awake, the'll be
No need to compromise
The next light, that we see
Will be the lights, of paradise

We should not fret
We're in good hands
And have been, all along

We'll walk the golden
Roads of peace
And sing a victor's song

Divine Intervention

When I was born
You took my hand
And helped me
From the womb

Then held me in
Your gentle arms
While I was cleansed
And groomed

And then you whispered to me
In my tiny, little ear
"It's time, for your life to begin
Walk child, but never fear,

For I will be with you, through all
Your perils, and your rain
I can not take it from you
But, my child, I'll ease your pain

And when you need a shoulder
I am never far away
But I must ask of you, one thing
That child, you learn to pray

For I'm your mighty, awesome Lord
And you are my, creation
I'll always keep you safe and warm
And far from, all temptation

And when your time,
On earth is through
You'll stand, right next to me
Together, we'll venture into

God's great eternity"

Words of Faith

Words of faith
Can take you higher
They have strength
And they inspire

They can change a doubter's day
And encourage, them to pray
Words of faith, can change a mind
Making them, leave sin behind

Turning their thoughts
To the pure
Making their hearts
Thirst for more

Words of faith
Are the soul's food
Gives a saint, more latitude
Makes them strong, in word and deed

For the gospel, they do heed
Words of faith
Can lift you up
Make you full, fill up your cup

Words of faith
Are from on high
Join the saints now
Don't be shy

So listen hard, and listen well
These precious words, are a good sell
And words of faith, they open doors
So come in now, and receive yours

The News Is Good

Folks, my cup it runneth over
And I have, so much to say
About our sweet Lord and savior
Yes, his word, his will, his way

I am here to spread the good word
That the Lord, will soon return
And I must remind the sinners
That for sure, they all will burn

There is no reward, for sinning
Just a sure and swift demise
For they were all, unrepentant
And a thorn in the Lord's, eyes

When he come we best, be ready
Have his house, in order too
For the master did intrust us
And he told us, what to do

Read the Bible, pray, fast, and believe
Do what's just and right and good
Live a blameless, peaceful, gentle life
Like a faithful Christian should

Clothe the poor, and feed the hungry
Praise the Lord, in all your days
When the master comes, he will be pleased
Reward you, in many ways

Then the heavens, will descend to earth
And so with it our great king
We will live forever with the Lord
And forever, laugh and sing.

The Volunteer

I am now in the Lord's army
And I am a volunteer
There is no doubt in my mind
That I will make this, my career

For the sovereign Lord, has blessed me
And now, he allows me to
Spread his light, and show his glory
And I know just, what to do

He has shown me how, to share my faith
His compassion, and his love
For my weapon, I am armed with care
My field jackets, lined with doves

For my breast plate, there is honor
My commander is, the truth
I will fight the war, on darkness
And attempt, to save our youth

For the fight for good and evil
Rages on, as I now speak
So I must defend the children
And I will protect, the weak

When it's time for me, to meet the Lord
He will say to me, well done
Then I'll take his warm, and loving hand
And we'll walk, into the sun

Encouragement
(For My Grandson Chris)

My son's problems will always be with us
For the devil has so many snares.
He will trap us and trip us whenever he can
If we're weak and we are unprepared.
But just take heart my son, you are favored
For the Lord God, He does have your back.
So no matter what Satan throws at you
From the Lord's blessings, you'll never lack.
See, the Lord will not remove our problems
But He will ease our burdens and pain.
So my son, be encouraged, not solemn or sad
For God will shelter you from the rain.
And remember when problems assail us,
They come only to make us much stronger.
Son, remember to pray and to praise the Lord God
For the devil won't be here much longer.
God has brought you this far.
He will not leave you now.
So please never feel that you're alone.
Broken bones, they will heal
For soon great you will feel
And your family will welcome you home.

Love always,

Grandma
(J. Green)
5/28/03

Love Professed

Lord I am yours, and yours alone
From only you, my life was sown
Since I was born
You held me close

I love you Lord
I love you most
No one but you, can give me breath
I'm here to serve, until my death

Lord it's you that I
Look up to
For guidance, love and life anew
I pray and praise you

With great zeal
You know my heart
And how I feel
And Lord, the day I see your face

I'll know that I am blessed with grace
Lord I know that
Your love is mine
And what you did

For all mankind
I will revere you, till I die
When I will meet you
In the sky.

Upstairs

Be encouraged, God is nigh
Pray to Jesus, don't be shy
For he stands right next to you
Filled with mercy, and love too

He's the answer to your prayers
Make room for the, man upstairs
In your heart and in your mind
Let his light from heaven shine

Place no one above the Lord
Then repent, and climb aboard
There's no worry, there's no shame
Make amends, then call his name

Full of mercy full of grace
For you now, he'll make a space
In his world of bliss and splendor
Just have faith, and then surrender

Rich will be, then your reward
For your blessings, they are stored
Come to him now, don't delay
With the Lord, then you will stay

Saving Grace

This girl talks, but she won't listen
To what others, have to say
Her words are much more important
Others' words, get in her way

She will not receive your comments
When she goes into her speal
It's as if the one, she talks with
Is not visible, or real

She is constantly complaining
About one thing or another
And there's no one who's her real friend
For she will not favor others

She won't ever call on God, unless
A problem should arise
She keeps all her cohorts' interests
With her gossip, and her lies

I had asked her one day if she
Would consider getting saved
When she questioned, saved from what
I thought her ignorant or brave

She says God is in her heart
But what spews out of her mouth
Only guarantees a ticket
On a train, that's going south

I will try hard to persuade her
From this dark and dismal place
And I'll ask the Lord, for strength
While I'm attempting to save grace

This task, it will not be easy
She is hardened to the core
I will pray for her, immortal soul
And the Lord, will do much more.

A Wonderful Day

There will be wars
And rumors of wars
There will be diseases
And now we have scars

Earthquakes and all sorts of
Natural disasters
Keep watching the skies
You may soon see, the master

There's murder and chaos
The third world's exploding
There's anger and death
And the devil's reloading

Homelessness, joblessness, on the increase
We must give all the credit
For this to the beast
But just as it seems

Things have gotten their worst
The Lord God, he will come
And his mercies, disperse
He will send satan running

Then clean up his mess
And then send him to hell
With great zeal, and great zest
All the liars and cheaters

The muggers, and thugs
Will be crushed under his foot
Like so many bugs
He will raise all the righteous

From their endless sleep
And give them new bodies
His promise, to keep
The wicked will be judged

And sent on their way
Then we all will join Jesus
What a wonderful day

Child of Light

A child of light
Is all aglow
For God he is on fire
He's so filled, with the holy ghost

That others, he inspires
He's kind and gentle
But he has, the strength
Of his convictions

With spiritual wisdom, at his hand
He's good at all predictions
A child of light, he is compassion
That's personified

He favors hope and goodness
For the Lord, is on his side
Through God, he will illuminate
Most anyone he meets

Yes from the high and mighty
To men living on the streets
You will know him, when you see him
He is smiling, and he's kind

So try to know this child of peace
For he is an awesome find.

Technology

We now are inundated
With the new technologies
The microwave, the cell phone
And the internet, are three

They cook your food, real fast
And you can talk, while anywhere
On the internet there's answers
Conversations, you can share

Now some folks use the internet
To seek and find, true love
From strangers they have never met
And know so little of

Folks, fall in love with Jesus first
It won't cost you a dime
His love is always free of charge
And he won't waste your time

Don't have to look a certain way
He says come as you are
Yes, give your life to Jesus
You'll be better off by far

Then when you learn, to obey God
And give your life to grace
He will provide a love for you
And you will know, his face

So don't go searching, round the world
For a romance to start
Repent your sins, accept the light
Let God into your heart

And then when it is time for you
To find your earthly love
The Lord will point him out to you
Love sanctioned, from above

About the Author

JOAN M. GREEN was born, raised, and educated in New York City. She has lived most of her life in Queens. She is one of seven children, to Lucille and Joseph Robinson, is a nurse by profession, and has been in nursing for many years. She gets most of her inspiration while working with her patients. As a matter of fact, ninety percent of her poetry is done while at work.

Joan M. Green loves animals. She owns two dogs, one named Barney, a golden retriever, and the other, Buddy, a mixed-breed. Being an admirer of natural things, she tries to keep her home reflective of the beauty of the outdoors. There you will find lots of green leafy plants, and three fish tanks, a thirty-gallon, a fifty-five gallon, and a ten-gallon. In the first two she has Oscars which she loves because they are intelligent, and they grow large. One of her Oscars she calls Mercy because he never ate the goldfish in the tank, and they will live together in harmony. She would love it if the world would take a lesson from them.

Being that she loves the outdoors and nature, she is a camping buff, and she also enjoys fishing and boating. Her favorite areas to visit are Bar Harbor, Maine, upstate New York, and the

Adirondacks. She loves these places because of their natural, unspoiled beauty.

Joan M. Green is a people person, and gets along with her fellow man very well. Last, but not least, she believes in the gospel of Jesus Christ, that He loves us all, and we are saved.